by Iain Gray

LangSyne
PUBLISHING
WRITING *to* REMEMBER

Lang**Syne**

PUBLISHING

WRITING *to* REMEMBER

79 Main Street, Newtongrange,
Midlothian EH22 4NA
Tel: 0131 344 0414   Fax: 0845 075 6085
E-mail: info@lang-syne.co.uk
www.langsyneshop.co.uk

Design by Dorothy Meikle
Printed by Printwell Ltd
© Lang Syne Publishers Ltd 2018

All rights reserved. No part of this publication may be reproduced, stored or introduced into a retrieval system, or transmitted in any form or by any means (electronic, mechanical, photocopying, recording or otherwise) without the prior written permission of Lang Syne Publishers Ltd.

ISBN 978-1-85217-295-4

Chapter one:
Origins of Irish surnames

According to an old saying, there are two types of Irish – those who actually are Irish and those who wish they were.

This sentiment is only one example of the allure that the high romance and drama of the proud nation's history holds for thousands of people scattered across the world today.

It's a sad fact, however, that the vast majority of Irish surnames are found far beyond Irish shores, rather than on the Emerald Isle itself.

The population stood at around eight million souls in 1841, but today it stands at fewer than six million.

This is mainly a tragic consequence of the potato famine, also known as the Great Hunger, which devastated Ireland between 1845 and 1849.

The Irish peasantry had become almost wholly reliant for basic sustenance on the potato, first introduced from the Americas in the seventeenth century.

When the crop was hit by a blight, at least 800,000 people starved to death while an estimated two million others were forced to seek a new life far from their native shores – particularly in America, Canada, and Australia.

The effects of the potato blight continued until about 1851, by which time a firm pattern of emigration had become established.

Ireland's loss, however, was to the gain of the countries in which the immigrants settled, contributing enormously, as their descendants do today, to the well being of the nations in which their forefathers settled.

But those who were forced through dire circumstance to establish a new life in foreign parts never forgot their roots, or the proud heritage and traditions of the land that gave them birth.

Nor do their descendants.

It is a heritage that is inextricably bound up in the colourful variety of Irish names themselves – and the origin and history of these names forms an integral part of the vibrant drama that is the nation's history, one of both glorious fortune and tragic misfortune.

This history is well documented, and one of the most important and fascinating of the earliest sources are *The Annals of the Four Masters*, compiled between 1632 and 1636 by four friars at the Franciscan Monastery in County Donegal.

Compiled from earlier sources, and purporting to go back to the Biblical Deluge, much of the material takes in the mythological origins and history of Ireland and the Irish.

This includes tales of successive waves of invaders and settlers such as the Fomorians, the Partholonians, the Nemedians, the Fir Bolgs, the Tuatha De Danann, and the Laigain.

Of particular interest are the *Milesian Genealogies*,

because the majority of Irish clans today claim a descent from either Heremon, Ir, or Heber – three of the sons of Milesius, a king of what is now modern day Spain.

These sons invaded Ireland in the second millennium B.C, apparently in fulfilment of a mysterious prophecy received by their father.

This Milesian lineage is said to have ruled Ireland for nearly 3,000 years, until the island came under the sway of England's King Henry II in 1171 following what is known as the Cambro-Norman invasion.

This is an important date not only in Irish history in general, but for the effect the invasion subsequently had for Irish surnames.

'Cambro' comes from the Welsh, and 'Cambro-Norman' describes those Welsh knights of Norman origin who invaded Ireland.

But they were invaders who stayed, inter-marrying with the native Irish population and founding their own proud dynasties that bore Cambro-Norman names such as Archer, Barbour, Brannagh, Fitzgerald, Fitzgibbon, Fleming, Joyce, Plunkett, and Walsh – to name only a few.

These 'Cambro-Norman' surnames that still flourish throughout the world today form one of the three main categories in which Irish names can be placed – those of Gaelic-Irish, Cambro-Norman, and Anglo-Irish.

Previous to the Cambro-Norman invasion of the twelfth century, and throughout the earlier invasions and settlement of those wild bands of sea rovers known as the Vikings in the eighth and ninth centuries, the population of the island was relatively small, and it was normal for a person to be identified through the use of only a forename.

But as population gradually increased and there were many more people with the same forename, surnames were adopted to distinguish one person, or one community, from another.

Individuals identified themselves with their own particular tribe, or 'tuath', and this tribe – that also became known as a clann, or clan – took its name from some distinguished ancestor who had founded the clan.

The Gaelic-Irish form of the name Kelly, for example, is Ó Ceallaigh, or O'Kelly, indicating descent from an original 'Ceallaigh', with the 'O' denoting 'grandson of.' The name was later anglicised to Kelly.

The prefix 'Mac' or 'Mc', meanwhile, as with the clans of the Scottish Highlands, denotes 'son of.'

Although the Irish clans had much in common with their Scottish counterparts, one important difference lies in what are known as 'septs', or branches, of the clan.

Septs of Scottish clans were groups who often bore an entirely different name from the clan name but were under the clan's protection.

In Ireland, septs were groups that shared the same name and who could be found scattered throughout the four provinces of Ulster, Leinster, Munster, and Connacht.

The 'golden age' of the Gaelic-Irish clans, infused as their veins were with the blood of Celts, pre-dates the Viking invasions of the eighth and ninth centuries and the Norman invasion of the twelfth century, and the sacred heart of the country was the Hill of Tara, near the River Boyne, in County Meath.

Known in Gaelic as 'Teamhar na Rí', or Hill of Kings, it was the royal seat of the 'Ard Rí Éireann', or High King of Ireland, to whom the petty kings, or chieftains, from the island's provinces were ultimately subordinate.

It was on the Hill of Tara, beside a stone pillar known as the Irish 'Lia Fáil', or Stone of Destiny, that the High Kings were inaugurated and, according to legend, this stone would emit a piercing screech that could be heard all over Ireland when touched by the hand of the rightful king.

The Hill of Tara is today one of the island's main tourist attractions.

Opposition to English rule over Ireland, established in the wake of the Cambro-Norman invasion, broke out frequently and the harsh solution adopted by the powerful forces of the Crown was to forcibly evict the native Irish from their lands.

These lands were then granted to Protestant colonists, or 'planters', from Britain.

Many of these colonists, ironically, came from Scotland and were the descendants of the original 'Scotti', or 'Scots', who gave their name to Scotland after migrating there in the fifth century A.D., from the north of Ireland.

Colonisation entailed harsh penal laws being imposed on the majority of the native Irish population, stripping them practically of all of their rights.

The Crown's main bastion in Ireland was Dublin and its environs, known as the Pale, and it was the dispossessed peasantry who lived outside this Pale, desperately striving to eke out a meagre living.

It was this that gave rise to the modern-day expression of someone or something being 'beyond the pale'.

Attempts were made to stamp out all aspects of the ancient Gaelic-Irish culture, to the extent that even to bear a Gaelic-Irish name was to invite discrimination.

This is why many Gaelic-Irish names were anglicised with, for example, and noted above, Ó Ceallaigh, or O'Kelly, being anglicised to Kelly.

Succeeding centuries have seen strong revivals of Gaelic-Irish consciousness, however, and this has led to many families reverting back to the original form of their name, while the language itself is frequently found on the fluent tongues of an estimated 90,000 to 145,000 of the island's population.

Ireland's turbulent history of religious and political strife is one that lasted well into the twentieth century, a landmark century that saw the partition of the island into the twenty-six counties of the independent Republic of

Ireland, or Eire, and the six counties of Northern Ireland, or Ulster.

Dublin, originally founded by Vikings, is now a vibrant and truly cosmopolitan city while the proud city of Belfast is one of the jewels in the crown of Ulster.

It was Saint Patrick who first brought the light of Christianity to Ireland in the fifth century A.D.

Interpretations of this Christian message have varied over the centuries, often leading to bitter sectarian conflict – but the many intricately sculpted Celtic Crosses found all over the island are symbolic of a unity that crosses the sectarian divide.

It is an image that fuses the 'old gods' of the Celts with Christianity.

All the signs from the early years of this new millennium indicate that sectarian strife may soon become a thing of the past – with the Irish and their many kinsfolk across the world, be they Protestant or Catholic, finding common purpose in the rich tapestry of their shared heritage.

Chapter two:
Warrior kings and adventurers

At least three sources can be traced for the presence of the proud name of Boyle in Ireland.

There are those Boyles who are of truly native Irish descent, those from Scotland, and those who settled there as lords and masters in the wake of the Anglo-Norman occupation of the island.

County Donegal, in the northwest of the Emerald Isle, was for centuries the territory of the powerful clan of Ó Baoighill, later anglicised as Boyle.

The founder of the clan was a mid to late tenth century Donegal chieftain known as Aneisleis O'Baoghail, with 'Baoghail' indicating 'having profitable pledges.'

In common with the O'Donnells and other clans who formed what was known as the Clan Conall of the northern Uí Neill, the Boyles traced a descent back to the legendary Niall Noíghiallach, better known to posterity as the great warrior king Niall of the Nine Hostages.

Niall became Ard Rí, or High King, in 379 A.D. and embarked on the series of military campaigns and other daring adventures that would subsequently earn him the title of Niall of the Nine Hostages.

The nine countries and territories into which he raided and took hostages for ransom were the Irish provinces of Munster, Leinster, Connacht, and Ulster, Britain, and the territories of the Saxons, Morini, Picts, and Dalriads.

Niall's most famous hostage was a young lad known as Succat, son of Calpernius, a Romano-Briton who lived in the area of present day Milford Haven, on the Welsh coast.

Later known as Patricius, or Patrick, he became renowned as Ireland's patron saint, St. Patrick, responsible for bringing the light of Christianity to the island in the early years of the fifth century A.D.

Raiding in Gaul, in the area of Boulogne-sur-mer in present day France, Niall was ambushed and killed by one of his treacherous subjects in 405A.D.

It was through Niall's son Conall Gulban that the Clan Conall was linked by blood to this most illustrious of Irish kings.

The ancient Boyle presence in Co. Donegal can still be found in place names, with Ballyweel, near the town of Donegal, originally known as Baile ui Bhaoighill, indicating 'the home of the O'Boyles.'

Only a few short miles across the sea from the northwest of Ireland, a family of Boyles had lived since the early years of the twelfth century in the Scottish west coast area of Ayrshire.

These Boyles were of original Norman stock, descended from lords and their retainers who had fought at the side of William the Conqueror at the battle of Hastings in 1066.

Their original name was de Boyville, taken from the place name of Beaville, in Normandy, from where they hailed.

In 1126, at the invitation of Scotland's David I, a number of this Norman nobility settled in Scotland.

Among them was Hugo de Morville, who was granted the lands of Cunningham and Largs; subsequently subdividing this territory he granted the lands of Kelburn to his close kinsfolk the de Boyvilles.

In common with the descendants of many other Norman settlers to Scotland, including the freedom fighter William Wallace and King Robert the Bruce, the de Boyvilles, or Boyles, soon became as Scottish as the native Scots, adopting the cause of what had become their Celtic homeland.

They fought at the side of Bruce in his victory over the army of England's Edward II at the battle of Bannockburn in 1314 and proved staunch supporters of the ill-fated Mary, Queen of Scots.

An earldom was bestowed on them in 1703, and the current clan chief of the Scottish Clan Boyle is the 10th Earl of Glasgow.

In the centuries following Scotland's Wars of Independence against England many Boyles settled in Ireland, particularly in the ancient northern province of

Ulster, and many of their descendants are to be found there to this day.

By far the biggest influx of 'foreign' Boyles to the island, however, came in the form of those Norman adventurers who acquired lands there in the bitter and bloody aftermath of the twelfth century Cambro-Norman invasion of the island and the subsequent consolidation of power by the English throne.

Ireland, in effect, became a vassal state of England, with the island ruled by an English elite behind the fortified walls of the city of Dublin and its environs.

One of the most prominent of the Anglo-Norman adventurers to lay claim to Irish soil was Richard Boyle, the father of a dynasty of famous and infamous Irish Boyles.

Born in 1566 in Canterbury, England, he left home for Ireland at the age of 22 to take advantage of the rich pickings in terms of lands and titles that were available to those ruthless enough to seize them.

He soon prospered, being appointed to a lucrative colonial government post only two years later and making an important marriage in 1595 to the daughter and co-heiress of William Apsley, a member of the council to the president of the province of the south-western province of Munster.

Boyle later fell foul of the envy of rivals and was falsely accused of fraud but, in 1600, after putting his case before England's Queen Elizabeth I, the monarch declared that he was 'a man fit to be employed by ourselves', and promptly appointed him clerk of the council of Munster.

Knighted in 1603, he was appointed a privy councillor for Ireland ten years later, and created Earl of Cork and Dungarven in 1620.

By 1631, having acquired vast estates along the way, including the 42,000 acre estate of the executed Sir Walter Raleigh in Co. Cork, he was appointed Lord High Treasurer of Ireland.

Known as 'The Great Earl of Cork' and 'the first colonial millionaire', Boyle had married his second wife, Catherine, following the death of his first wife in 1599.

The couple had no less than eight daughters and eleven sons – and some of these sons went on to play prominent roles not only in Irish affairs but further afield.

While some of the original native Gaelic Irish families had been reluctantly forced to seek an accommodation of sorts with the English Crown over the centuries, others found themselves drawn into insurrection and rebellion.

In 1641 landowners such as the native Irish Boyles and the O'Donnells of Co. Donegal rebelled against the English Crown's policy of settling, or 'planting' loyal Protestants on Irish land.

This policy had started during the reign from 1491 to 1547 of Henry VIII, whose Reformation effectively outlawed the established Roman Catholic faith throughout his dominions.

In the insurrection that exploded in 1641, at least 2,000 Protestant settlers were massacred and thousands more were stripped of their belongings and driven from their lands to seek refuge where they could.

England had its own distractions with the Civil War that culminated in the execution of Charles I in 1649, and from 1641 to 1649 Ireland was ruled by a rebel group known as the Irish Catholic Confederation, or the Confederation of Kilkenny.

Richard Boyle, 1st Earl of Cork, became an early victim of the rebellion – being chased off his lands and dying two years later.

A monument erected by the earl in his lifetime to himself, his mother, his wives, and his children can be seen today in St Mary's Church, in Youghal, Co. Cork, while another imposing monument can be see in Dublin's St. Mary's Cathedral.

Following their father's death, his sons were destined to play a bloody role in suppressing the rebellion, managing to recover their landed heritage in full.

But the brutal suppression of the rebellion, largely at the hands of England's 'Lord Protector' Oliver Cromwell, who descended on the island at the head of a 20,000-strong army in August of 1649, would have dire consequences for clans such as the Boyles of Donegal.

Chapter three:

High honours

The third surviving son of the 1st Earl of Cork, Roger Boyle, known as 'The Wise', born in 1621 and who later held the titles of 1st Earl of Orrery and Baron of Broghill, first clashed arms with the Confederate rebels at the battle of Liscarrol in September of 1642.

At his side was his brother Richard Boyle, later 1st Earl of Burlington, 2nd Earl of Cork, and 1st Baron Clifford of Lanesborough.

The Royalists achieved a victory over the rebels at Liscarrol, but Roger Boyle was to achieve a much more decisive victory over them nine years later at the battle of Knocknaclashy.

By this time he was fighting on the side of the Parliamentary army of Oliver Cromwell.

On May 10, 1650 Boyle defeated an Irish force that had been marching to the relief of Cork at the battle of Macroom.

By this time now firm friends with Cromwell, he was entrusted with what proved to be the final defeat of the rebel leader Donagh McCarthy, Viscount Muskerry, who was marching at the head of a 3000-strong army to attempt to relieve the besieged defenders of Limerick.

Cromwell earlier had remarked of Boyle's father, the 1st

Earl of Cork, that 'if there had been an Earl of Cork in every province it would have been impossible for the Irish to have raised a rebellion.'

It was at Knocknaclashy, near the village of Banteer, that in July of 1651 Boyle intercepted Viscount Muskerry's numerically superior force.

Although outnumbered, Boyle's force was better equipped and trained, and he directed the battle that led to the virtual slaughter of Muskerry's brave but doomed infantry and cavalry.

Boyle lost less than 30 dead and only 130 wounded.

Nursing a burning hatred for the rebels, Boyle ordered that all prisoners should be killed – except those of 'quality' who would fetch a fair ransom.

Later giving an account of the slaughter, Boyle related how Catholic charms, assuring that the wearer would be impervious to weapons, were found sewn into the ragged clothing of the rebel dead.

Viscount Muskerry and what remained of his army retreated in great confusion to Ross Castle, where they were forced into humiliating surrender the following year.

The battle proved to be the final death knell of the rebellion, with Cromwell already having initiated a policy of what amounted to ethnic cleansing.

His troopers were given free rein to hunt down and kill priests, while all Catholic estates were confiscated.

Catholic landowners such as the Boyles of Donegal

were grudgingly given pathetically small estates west of the river Shannon – where they were hemmed in by colonies of Cromwellian soldiers.

Many Gaelic-Irish such as the Boyles of Donegal were later forced to seek a new life in foreign lands – where their descendants flourish to this day.

Created Earl of Orrery and appointed a lord justice of Ireland in 1660, Boyle later gained fame as a statesman and dramatist – his literary works, perhaps fittingly, including his 1677 *Treatise of the Art of War*.

Other products of his pen were the plays *The Black Prince* and *Tryphon*.

His brother Richard, 2nd Earl of Cork, after various vacillations in his loyalties, was appointed a privy councillor and Lord Treasurer of Ireland in 1660 following the Restoration of Charles II.

In 1689, following the flight of James II and the subsequent accession to the thrones of England, Scotland, and Ireland of the Protestant William of Orange and his wife Mary, James held a Parliament in Dublin that effectively confiscated the estates of Protestants such as Boyle.

But William later overturned this, and the Boyle estates were secured.

Henry Boyle, a grandson of Roger Boyle, 1st Earl of Orrery, was created Earl of Shannon in 1756; his son, the second earl, who was a Vice-Treasurer for Ireland, was created Baron Carleton in 1786.

The titles are still retained by the family.

Meanwhile not all of the 1st Earl of Cork's sons were to be found on the battlefields of Ireland.

Born in Lismore Castle in Co. Waterford in 1627, Robert Boyle was the seventh son of the earl and is remembered today as 'The Father of Chemistry.'

Also known as Robert Boyle 'The Philosopher' he was something of a child prodigy, learning to speak French, Greek, and Latin at an early age.

Educated at Eton and later travelling to France, Switzerland, and Italy, he returned to England in 1645 to settle in the Boyle family manor of Stalbridge, in Dorset, that had been bequeathed to him by his father.

Dedicating himself to a life of intensive scientific research, he became a member of the group of fellow seekers of knowledge known as the Invisible College, forerunner of the scientific 'think-tank', the Royal Society.

By 1654 he was settled in Oxford, and it was here that he dabbled in alchemy – the attempt to turn base metals into gold.

It was partly due to these albeit abortive experiments, that Boyle made a number of important scientific discoveries – including what is known today as Boyle's Law, that 'the volume of a gas varies inversely as the pressure upon it, providing temperature is constant.'

In addition to other important discoveries in the realms of chemistry and physics, Boyle studied theology and spent a great deal of his wealth on promoting the spread of Christianity throughout the territory of the East India Company, of which he was a director.

It is also thanks to Robert Boyle that Boyles of today can boast a place name on the moon – this is Boyle Crater, the lunar impact crater named in his honour.

Meanwhile in art, Richard Boyle, 3rd Earl of Burlington, 4th Earl of Cork, and known as 'the architect earl' was born in Yorkshire in 1694.

A direct descendant of Richard Boyle, 1st Earl of Cork, he was responsible for the design of not only his own London residence of Burlington House in Piccadilly, but also the York Assembly Rooms and Tottenham Park, in Wiltshire.

Chapter four:
On the world stage

The recipient of a number of prestigious awards for his comedic and dramatic roles Peter Boyle, born in 1935 in Norristown, Pennsylvania, and who died in 2006, was the American actor who from 1996 to 2005 played the role of Frank Barone in the popular U.S. sitcom *Everybody Loves Raymond*.

He is also remembered as the singing and dancing monster in the 1977 horror film spoof *Young Frankenstein*.

He won an Emmy Award in 1996 for a guest-starring role in the science fiction drama *The X Files*, while he was also a recipient of a Screen Actors Guild Award.

Born in 1970 in Davenport, Iowa, **Lara Flynn Boyle** is the American actress whose film roles include the 1986 *Ferris Bueller's Day Off*, *Amerika*, the 1989 *Dead Poet's Society*, and the 2007 *Have Dreams Will Travel*.

She has also played the role of Donna Hayward in the critically acclaimed television series *Twin Peaks*.

Behind the camera lens **Danny Boyle** is the British director and producer who was born in 1956 in Radcliffe, Lancashire, and whose many film credits include the 1994 *Shallow Grave*, the 1996 *Trainspotting*, and *28 Days Later*, from 2007.

The recipient in 2008 of an Honorary Academy Award

in recognition of one of cinema's great careers in art direction, **Robert F. Boyle** is the veteran American art director and production designer who was born in Los Angeles in 1909.

Best known for his work as production designer for a number of Alfred Hitchcock films that include *North by North West* (1949) and the 1963 *The Birds*, he is also the recipient of an Art Directors Guild's Lifetime Achievement Award.

The daughter of an Italian marquis, the grandly named Caterina Irene Elena Maria Imperiala DiFrancavilla is better known as the television presenter **Katy Boyle**, born in Florence in 1926.

At one time married to Viscount Boyle, now Earl of Shannon, she appeared in the 1960s on popular British television shows such as *What's My Line?* and *Juke Box Jury*, while she also presented the Eurovision Song Contest in the 1960s and 1970s.

In the world of comedy **Frankie Boyle**, born in Glasgow in 1972, is the Scottish comedian whose British television appearances include popular shows such as *Mock the Week*, *8 out of 10 Cats*, and *Would I Lie To You?*

Generations of Boyles have also gained distinction on the battlefield, not least English-born **Edward Boyle**, who was awarded the Victoria Cross, the highest award for gallantry for British and Commonwealth forces.

Born in 1883, he was a Lieutenant-Commander in the

Royal Navy during the First World War when, in command of a submarine in the Sea of Marmara in the Dardanelles in April of 1915, he sank two Turkish gunboats and one military transport.

This was achieved despite navigational difficulties, strong currents, and a number of enemy naval patrols; later promoted to the rank of Rear Admiral, he died in 1967.

Also at sea **Thomas Boyle**, born in 1775 at Marblehead, Massachusetts, had been a daring privateer before becoming an officer in the United States Navy in 1812.

The U.S. Naval vessel U.S.S. Boyle and Boyle Street in Baltimore are both named in his honour.

A brigadier general with the Union Army during the American Civil War of 1861 to 1865, **Jeremiah Boyle** was born in 1818 in what was then Mercer County, Kentucky; the county was later named Boyle County in honour of his father, **Chief Justice John Boyle**.

A practising lawyer before the outbreak of war, Jeremiah Boyle was in favour of the gradual emancipation of slaves and argued for such as a delegate to the Kentucky State Constitutional Convention in 1849.

Commissioned as a brigadier general shortly after the outbreak of the Civil War, Boyle fought at the battle of Shiloh and in May of 1862 was appointed military governor of Kentucky.

His son **Colonel William Boyle**, the youngest officer

to hold such rank in the Union Army, was killed in action at the battle of Marion, in Tennessee.

At the end of the war Boyle became a successful land speculator and was instrumental in the setting up of a street railway system in Louisville, Kentucky, before his death in 1871.

Taking to the air **Sir Dermot Boyle**, born in Ireland in 1904 and educated in Dublin, became a Marshall of Britain's Royal Air Force, commanding No.83 Squadron during the Second World War and serving as Chief of the Air Staff from 1956 to 1959.

He died in 1993.

Boyles have also excelled in the highly competitive world of sport.

Born in Melbourne in 1951, **Raelene Boyle** is the former Australian athlete who is the proud owner of three Olympic silver medals.

She took silver for the 200-metre sprint at the 1968 Olympics in Mexico City and silver medals for the 100-metre and 200-metre sprints at the 1972 Munich Olympics.

Also the winner of seven gold and two silver medals at Commonwealth Games, she was awarded an M.B.E. in 1974, named one of the National Trust of Australia's 'National Treasures' in 1998, and made a Member of the Order of Australia in 2007.

Nicknamed 'Honest Jack' and born in Cincinnati in

1866, **John Boyle** was a noted American catcher and first baseman in Major League Baseball, while **Henry J. Boyle**, born in Philadelphia in 1860, was a catcher with the St. Louis Maroons and the Indianapolis Hoosiers.

Also in baseball **Jimmy 'Browntown' Boyle**, born in 1904 in Cincinnati and who died in 1958, was the catcher for the New York Giants in 1926 who later established the famous New York steakhouse known as The Browntown Beefery.

In the ecclesiastical sphere **Father Leonard Boyle** was the Irish-Canadian scholar in palaeography and medieval studies who served as Prefect for the Vatican Library from 1984 to 1997.

Born in 1923 in Ballintra, Co. Donegal, he later moved to Toronto where he taught for a time at the Pontifical Institute of Medieval Studies at Toronto University.

He died in 1999, twelve years after being made an Officer of the Order of Canada.

Born in 1873 in Johnstown, Pennsylvania, **Hugh Boyle** served as Roman Catholic Archbishop of Pittsburgh from 1921 to 1950, while **Cardinal Patrick O'Boyle**, born in Scranton, Pennsylvania, in 1896 served as Archbishop of Washington from 1947 to 1973.

In the world of literature T. Coraghessan Boyle, better known as **T.C. Boyle**, is the American short story writer and novelist who was born in 1948 in Peekshill, New York.

A distinguished professor of English at the University of Southern California since 1978, his many works include the 1987 *World's End*, *The Road to Wellville* (1993), and the 2006 *Talk Talk*.

Born in 1902 in St. Paul, Minnesota, **Kay Boyle** was the leading American writer and political activist who was a member of the American Academy of Arts and Letters and the recipient of two Guggenheim Fellowships, and a Lifetime Achievement Award from the National Endowment for the Arts.

Her works include the 1936 novel *Death of a Man*, which warned of the growing threat of Nazism, and the 1993 *Winter Night*.

She was also an active supporter of Amnesty International until her death in 1992.

In the world of art **Jimmy Boyle** is the Scottish sculptor who was born in the Gorbals area of Glasgow in 1944.

Once recognised as 'the most violent man in Scotland', he had been serving a term of imprisonment for murder in a special unit of Glasgow's Barlinnie Prison when he turned his hand to sculpture.

Following his release from prison in 1980 he has successfully pursued a career as both a sculptor and a writer.

Also born in Glasgow **Mark Boyle**, born in 1934, was the innovative artist who, along with his partner Joan Hills and their children Georgia and Sebastian, exhibited as The Boyle Family.

Boyle, who died in 2005, was also famous for the pioneering light shows he staged in the 1960s for performances of rock stars such as Jim Hendrix and Soft Machine.

In politics **John Boyle**, born in 1871 in Sykestown, Ontario, served as leader of the Alberta Liberal Party from 1922 to 1924 before being appointed to the Supreme Court of Alberta.

The Edmonton neighbourhood of Boyle Street and the village of Boyle, Alberta, are named in his honour.

Boyles have also made a significant contribution to the field of medicine.

Born in 1875 in Barbados, **Henry Boyle** was the pioneering anaesthesiologist who gave his name to the anaesthesia machine he devised for administering general anaesthesia and which is known as Boyle's Machine.

Boyles have also produced their fair share of adventurers, no less so than the Canadian Joseph Whiteside Boyle, born in 1867 and who was better known as **Klondike Joe Boyle**.

Amassing a fortune from gold mining in the Klondike, he organised a machine-gun company, later incorporated into the Canadian Army, to fight on the battlefields of France and Belgium during the First World War.

He was also responsible during the war for managing

to persuade Russia's Bolshevik government to return the Romanian Crown Jewels to Romania, and was later awarded the title of 'Saviour of Romania.'

He died and was buried in Middlesex, England, in 1923, but was re-interred fifty years later in his hometown of Woodstock, Ontario.

Speculation still abounds to this day as to whether or not the bold Klondike Joe had been involved in a love affair with the Romanian Queen, Marie of Edinburgh, a granddaughter of Queen Victoria.

Key dates in Ireland's history from the first settlers to the formation of the Irish Republic:

circa 7000 B.C.	Arrival and settlement of Stone Age people.
circa 3000 B.C.	Arrival of settlers of New Stone Age period.
circa 600 B.C.	First arrival of the Celts.
200 A.D.	Establishment of Hill of Tara, Co. Meath, as seat of the High Kings.
circa 432 A.D.	Christian mission of St. Patrick.
800-920 A.D.	Invasion and subsequent settlement of Vikings.
1002 A.D.	Brian Boru recognised as High King.
1014	Brian Boru killed at battle of Clontarf.
1169-1170	Cambro-Norman invasion of the island.
1171	Henry II claims Ireland for the English Crown.
1366	Statutes of Kilkenny ban marriage between native Irish and English.
1529-1536	England's Henry VIII embarks on religious Reformation.
1536	Earl of Kildare rebels against the Crown.
1541	Henry VIII declared King of Ireland.
1558	Accession to English throne of Elizabeth I.
1565	Battle of Affane.
1569-1573	First Desmond Rebellion.
1579-1583	Second Desmond Rebellion.
1594-1603	Nine Years War.
1606	Plantation' of Scottish and English settlers.
1607	Flight of the Earls.
1632-1636	Annals of the Four Masters compiled.
1641	Rebellion over policy of plantation and other grievances.
1649	Beginning of Cromwellian conquest.
1688	Flight into exile in France of Catholic Stuart monarch James II as Protestant Prince William of Orange invited to take throne of England along with his wife, Mary.
1689	William and Mary enthroned as joint monarchs; siege of Derry.
1690	Jacobite forces of James defeated by William at battle of the Boyne (July) and Dublin taken.

1691	Athlone taken by William; Jacobite defeats follow at Aughrim, Galway, and Limerick; conflict ends with Treaty of Limerick (October) and Irish officers allowed to leave for France.
1695	Penal laws introduced to restrict rights of Catholics; banishment of Catholic clergy.
1704	Laws introduced constricting rights of Catholics in landholding and public office.
1728	Franchise removed from Catholics.
1791	Foundation of United Irishmen republican movement.
1796	French invasion force lands in Bantry Bay.
1798	Defeat of Rising in Wexford and death of United Irishmen leaders Wolfe Tone and Lord Edward Fitzgerald.
1800	Act of Union between England and Ireland.
1803	Dublin Rising under Robert Emmet.
1829	Catholics allowed to sit in Parliament.
1845-1849	The Great Hunger: thousands starve to death as potato crop fails and thousands more emigrate.
1856	Phoenix Society founded.
1858	Irish Republican Brotherhood established.
1873	Foundation of Home Rule League.
1893	Foundation of Gaelic League.
1904	Foundation of Irish Reform Association.
1913	Dublin strikes and lockout.
1916	Easter Rising in Dublin and proclamation of an Irish Republic.
1917	Irish Parliament formed after Sinn Fein election victory.
1919-1921	War between Irish Republican Army and British Army.
1922	Irish Free State founded, while six northern counties remain part of United Kingdom as Northern Ireland, or Ulster; civil war up until 1923 between rival republican groups.
1949	Foundation of Irish Republic after all remaining constitutional links with Britain are severed.